I0150522

Life Through The Eyes Of A Poet !

Robert L. Fox

Life Through The Eyes Of A Poet !

ISBN 978-0-6151-8589-7

Life Through The Eyes Of A Poet

Copyright: © 2008 Robert L. Fox Standard Copyright License

All rights reserved. Except for use in review, the reproduction or utilization of this work in whole or in part in any form by any electronic, mechanical or other means, now known or hereafter invented, including xerography, photocopying and recording, or in any information storage or retrieval system, is forbidden without written permission from the Author/Publisher Robert L. Fox

Preface!

What brings us to this place? Is it destiny?

Has our life been set forth by a power beyond our control?

Do we control what is to be or where we will go?

Is it merely coincidence or something else?

We are born into this world and brought up by those around us. Being taught all the things that will get us through this life. Constantly learning new things about life and ourselves each and everyday. Yet there are times I'm not too sure about whether or not we have any control. People we meet places we go some that we feel a close bond too. I feel that everyone we meet has a role to play in our lives. Places that we go are almost like we have to go there.

I do not have the answers to questions we all have asked but I hope that my poetry may enlighten your heart and soul if only for a moment. This very world we live in is in constant turmoil due to religious differences as well as racial tension. Yet no one tries to change it for the better only expressing what they want to believe. I am not here to judge anyone and yet I myself have fallen into that trend due to others around me.

Let this world be our legacy of how we strived to do what is right not how much we hated everything that was here. The poetry I've written in the following pages of this book are meant to express my views on life and how I feel about various aspects of that. Not meant to discourage or lead astray from what you believe in. Please enjoy!

Robert L. Fox

Poetry List

6. A wish for the world
7. After Life
9. An Ode To Truck Drivers
10. Another Day
11. Another Tomorrow
12. Beginnings
13. Changing
14. Childhood
15. Cities
16. Creation
17. Dad
18. Daddy
20. Doctors
21. Eagles of our Skies
22. Earth Mother Of All
23. Fall
24. Finally
25. For My DJ named J
26. Forever Yours
27. Happiness Is Love
28. Have We Come To The End
29. How Long
30. How Will It End
31. Just A Smile
32. Let The Music Flow
33. Life Has Changed
34. Life Missed
35. Love
36. Mans Ingenuity
37. Mother
38. Natures Echoes
39. Night Fall
40. Now
41. Nurses
42. Ode To A Great Oak
43. Of Things Gone By
44. Release
45. Rivers Of Life

Peaceful days and nights ahead for everyone,
Finally ending the need for wars and guns,
Wouldn't that be a lovely thing to behold,
For all the generations unborn to grow up to;

A life full of lovely days without fears of wars,
Living for the best of all things created,
Beauty brought forth in nature trees ,flowers and such,
To be able to bloom without being destroyed;

Snow as pure as it can be falling down on mother earth,
Streams flowing clear and unpolluted one could drink from,
Stacks from mills emitting no pollutants into the air,
Cars and trucks burning fuel cleanly and efficiently;

Everyone getting along with their neighbors,
Whether near or far, living in harmony with the earth,
Helping their fellow man when in need of anything,
Reaching out to others around the world to help;

Wouldn't that be a wondrous thing to happen,
How grand it would be for all of us to live in harmony,
Just think of the great achievements that could take place,
If everyone worked together to make this a better world;

Break of dawn and here I stand
Looking out over the land
Pondering the life I've led
Thinking now that it was one I dread.

Looking back over the past
I catch a glimpses of love at last
Raising up from times gone bye
I glance lovingly to the sky.

Remembrances of good times and bad
Remind me of things I've had
Ever wondering in my mind
Just what will happen in the end of my time.

Will I see the things I've done
Good or bad that become one
With the vision of my life
I've never known anything but strife.

But that's not true because I've known
Many souls have come and gone
Touching me in times of sorrow
Reminding me there's always tomorrow.

I search the fields of life before
Opening each and every door
Looking for the pathway there
Without a worry or a care.

This never ending road I'm on
Will not forever go on and on
A day will come when I must pass
Into the other realm of eternity at last.

This place we all dread to go
Lies waiting there outside the door
I know it will open one day soon
For all to enter into the gloom.

But that could be a fearful sight
Except for the eternal light
The belief passed down through life.

8

Is the only hope that remains in life.

That there is eternal peace for those who seek
The path of righteousness for the meek
Never giving in to that awful fear
That nothing really awaits us after here!

How beautiful a land we live in,
Open prairies and forest abundant with life,
From the smallest of streams to raging rivers,
Flowing endlessly to the sea from their beginnings;

Cities as small as a house or two.
To so large it takes an hour to drive through,
Roads covered by trees above,
To double lanes with overpasses above;

Always traveling through this great land,
Truck Drivers of all races and nations do stand,
Delivering all the things we use,
Everyday including our daily refuse;

Weekends while we play and sleep,
Drivers travel up and down our streets,
Upon their way to your local store,
Their freight backed in to the door;

Without this breed of drivers vast,
Our lives would simply cease to last,
The clothes we wear and foods we eat,
Brought to us by great big fleets;

Things we cook with, TV's to watch,
Cars we drive and Boats or Yachts,
Houses, Bridges, Buildings of great heights,
Brought by truck drivers to these sites;

Without truckers what would we do,
They bring everything for me and you,
To have the life we've come to know,
So that our lives can smoothly flow;

Yet another day and so many things have changed,
Another day and the same thing gets rearranged,
Following the path I find there is beauty everywhere,
Also there is profound wisdom for those who choose to care.

What holds us here in our life of pain and sorrow,
What holds us here as if there's no tomorrow,
Does it matter if the sun comes up in the morning,
Does it make a difference to any of those in mourning.

Oh! If only tomorrow would bring joy to all,
As the beauty of a warm day late in the fall,
Whispering wind blowing through the trees,
Fills my heart with gladness, puts my mind at ease.

Where does it take us and when will it end,
Another day of life gone bye yet another to begin,
Swept away in the hustle of every day you are,
Reaching out for something to believe in from afar.

Wandering through this world you seek to find,
What is waiting there in the shadows of your mind,
You have to face the days one by one as they come,
Another day to ponder what there is to overcome.

Feel free to boldly question everything that is new,
But don't forget to see it when it comes back to you,
For things are not always as they seem or appear to be,
You have to find the answer in all the things you see!

Everyday there is something new,
Places to go and things to do,
People traveling to and fro,
Heading for another tomorrow;

No matter what mother nature can do,
We still keep going as if to renew,
Our very reason to live out our lives,
Regardless of how much pain or strife;

Turn on the T.V. or Radio, listen to the news
Of another disaster or person abused,
Nations may rise and they may fall,
But throughout this world we stand tall;

For whenever there is a reason to believe,
We all pull together for those in such need,
Fighting among ourselves doesn't matter much,
When others are dying without much of a fuss;

Families and friends all come together,
Whenever others lives are destroyed by man or weather,
Then we truly see how strong we are as a nation,
When help pours in without any hesitation;

God bless all those who help out in these times,
For without them our lives would fall by the waysides,
Forgotten forever with no one to care,
Thanks so much for all those that share;

How it must have been in those beginning days,
Land rising towards the heavens and falling into pits,
Entire continents rising from the waters of this world,
To form the very place we now live to this day;

As I drive all over this great land I try to recall,
How that must have looked before the great thaw,
An ice riddled plain valleys carved so deep,
From receding glaciers o'er the land they scraped;

Mountains thrust up towards the sky,
Land left almost flat for hundreds of miles,
Folded, twisted, ground up and such,
How violent all that must have been;

Cracks and crevasses oh so deep,
No one could fathom where they reach,
Rivers flowing from lakes anew,
Where before there were none in view;

Now divided by oceans vast,
Our lands once joined in the distant past,
Ice caps both on the north and south,
To keep the water levels balanced;

Heat and cold blow cross the land,
Bring changes to the place we stand,
So much has happened since the world began,
Yet there is much we need to understand;

Shifts in time or in the sand,
And things perish throughout the land,
Wind and rain, fire and ice,
Bring forth the things in our paradise;

How much I've changed since I was young,
Had no worries and lot's of fun,
Watching the sky late at night,
Looking up at the heavens with delight;

Amazed by the very sight,
Of all these stars in the night,
How can it be that this is the only one,
Where life like ours had begun;

Somewhere perhaps we'll see,
Another world where we could be,
Lets just hope that if this is true,
They have more compassion than me and you;

Just look at all the things we do,
To change the world to suit me and you,
Tear down trees and mountain tops,
Just to build new parking lots;

Dig big holes into the land,
To dump the trash from our garbage cans,
Build higher buildings than before,
To show the world that we're not poor;

Yet on our streets there lives our poor,
No money for food from the Grocery store,
Lost their lives of working steady,
Because of things they were not ready;

Yet there they stay for no one cares,
Due to nothing but our fears,
Maybe we just can't seem to admit,
There is a problem that can be fixed;

Where have you gone that time of carefree pleasures,
Playing in the snow never giving thought to the cold,
Sledding, Ice Skating, never once realizing how cold we were,
Building snow forts and snow ball fights in the pouring snow,

Playing hide and seek with all your friends in the area,
Running to an fro never growing tired or hungry,
Climbing trees and hiding in the tall grass of a field,
Playing army and waiting in your foxhole hidden from view,

Playing ball in the heat of the day not caring how hot it is,
Not once giving in to the sun over head or the mild shower,
Chasing butterflies in the field, or June bugs to play with,
Playing and running with your dog or playing catch with friends,

Now and then I catch a glimpses of these things in my children,
Then later on in the Grandchildren only to wonder,
Was I that full of energy never getting tired of playing,
Thinking where do they get the energy to keep going,

That moment in time when all the things we did as children comes back,
Amazed at how little we remember till that moment,
Shocked at how old we've become and how easily we tire now,
If only we could retain the power of youth we'd never grow old!!

15   Cities!

For my wife and daughter's support and encouragement!

I remember you from days before;
I walked your streets, looked in your stores;
I've seen your statues and sites;
That which was upon your shores;

The land lovely, and full of life;
The people friendly, not full of strife;
Openly I came to know how you are;
Only to find things not looked for;

For like all places around this world;
There is a dark side in shadows and void;
A place where others seem to hide;
Those with empty faces without pride;

This undertow of people gone bad;
Hidden in shadows of darkness and dread;
They prey upon those trying so hard;
To keep their lives happy and never be bad;

It matters not where on this world you go;
Those same faces seem to come also;
Whatever possessed them to follow that path;
So deep into darkness they never come back.

Creation!

Oh how miniscule we are in the void of darkness;
Floating endlessly through space;
Adrift on our journey to who knows where or when;
Searching and never seeing the reality of life;

Seeking knowledge of forever, being just out of reach;
Hoping for an answer, but not really wanting one;
Hoping there's a Heaven, praying there's no Hell;
Wanting forgiveness, but never forgiving;

So small we are in this vastness of space & time;
Even our size matters not outside this sphere;
How are we to understand that which we cannot see;
When we cannot understand that which we can see;

Is there a sureness of how or by whom we were created;
Does it really matter to anyone but those who ask;
I think not, for they seek that which no one can explain;
Nor can it be proven to their satisfaction;

That which we choose to believe is reality;
To those who venture outside this realm;
Step into the darkness without fear;
For we may find light instead of darkness there!!

Dad!

Here it is again approaching that one day of the year,
When all fathers share in the fullness of cheer,
Children born and growing or grown,
Remember you on this day of your own.

I remember back years before when Dad was working,
Never giving thought to his own needs or work to be shirking,
Bring home the necessary things that the family needed,
Food and shelter and our clothes in this he succeeded.

We had hard times that's true but through it all,
Our Father never once let us fall,
There were times I'm sure he grew tired of it all,
Yet he continued on through winter till fall.

A more devoted man we could not ask,
Seems as though he could do most any task,
Fixed my bike, and mended the fence,
Kept the car running and came to our defense.

Taught us things we needed to know,
To make our own lives seemingly flow,
Always wanting the very best for us in life,
Encouraging us all to learn and deal with strife.

How much I owe you for all that you gave,
How Long we looked for what our hearts craved,
You were there through it all with head held high,
I'll always love you for those years gone bye.

Never again will you be there through thick and thin,
But all that you taught me has remained within,
Grown now with family too, remembering all you went through,
The lessons over how well I learned, thank you Dad with love anew!!

Daddy!
Requiem for A Father

Not only a Father but a Husband of many years,
Working together they raised a family of seven,
Struggling at times but never giving up,
Through hardships and good times they stuck it out;

Mother providing the care and nurturing as only she could,
Father providing the necessities of his children,
Together always working through their problems,
Sometime easily and sometimes not, but never giving in;

Father how good it was to know you,
It was you who helped bring us into this world,
You who taught us what was needed to survive,
How to stand up for ourselves and fight;

You were there to teach us right from wrong,
How to think, not what to think,
How to stand strong but yet bend to a child,
Enjoyed working with your hands to create;

Always there with a shoulder to cry on,
Or an outstretched arm to hold us when we hurt,
Also there when we did wrong,
With a smack on the butt or a lecture;

How hard you worked long hours with low pay,
Yet you continued to put all of us first over yourself,
Didn't matter how tired or wore out you were,
The provider of our daily needs and protector of all;

Never mattered day or night if we needed you,
You were there and willing to help us out in our hour of need,
Glad to meet our spouses whether you really liked them or not,
Ready to respond if someone got hurt to assist anyway you could;

Always the first to ask if everything was alright,
Never giving though to your own needs,
If someone else was in trouble,
Always showing us you loved us;

Even if you didn't like what we were doing at the time,
Funny how we never noticed you growing older,

Guess we never wanted it to end,
But then life has a way of bringing us back to reality;

The years spent knowing you will never be forgotten,
The love you gave as well as the knowledge you gave,
Will always remain in our hearts as long as we're alive,
The passion you showed for things in life will always live on;

Above all things I am glad that you are finally at peace,
No longer hurting and grasping for straws,
But going on to a better place where friends await you,
We will carry your loving memory forever in our hearts;

With love now and forever till we meet again we love you and will miss you.

Colds and flu , fevers and such ,
We want too have a doctors touch,
Heal the sick and cure our ill's,
Then we all complain about bills;

The years of study they must do,
Just to help take care of me and you,
Learning for some it never ends,
As medicines and procedures change;

So do their practices have to be rearranged,
Ever trying to achieve a better way to treat our needs,
A heart full of true concern they have,
To heal us with the knowledge at hand;

Steady how their hands must be,
In order to perform all surgeries,
How hard it must become ,
When it doesn't help someone;

Spending hours of time to make them well,
A task that's hard when things can fail,
Long hours are spent by these men and women,
Just to hear us complain and tell them our symptoms;

I myself am glad they are here,
Would like to thank them for my life so dear,
Perhaps if others understood,
Then seeing them would always be good;

How beautiful you soar above the canyons floor,
Gliding through the air so swiftly like a mighty roar,
Wingtips barely moving as you catch another gust,
Of the winds higher up that come up in a rush;

Barely can I see you there floating up so high,
At times now just a speck I see weaving in the sky,
Suddenly I see you tilt and fall at breakneck speed,
To catch the prey you spotted so you can feed your breed;

How amazing that you can see them from great heights,
Then swoop down upon them and catch them while in flight,
I guess that's why they call you the King of birds that fly,
Always on patrol you are the Eagle of our American sky's;

How long you have comforted me in my journey through this realm,
Provided me with shelter from the storm and cold winds that blow,
Gave me nourishment when I became hungry, waters to quench my thirst,
Showered me with the beauty off all things created to enjoy in your realm:

The flowers of various colors and sizes, trees to reach the sky or swing on,
Green grass cool to the touch and warm to the heart in the warmth of the sun,
Golden fields of wheat reaching across the plains as far as the eye can see,
Majestic mountains so high we could not see the tops from up close;

Clouds as white as snow or grey filled with the rains of nourishment for all living things,
Rivers of all sizes from great flowing masses of water to small babbling streams through meadows,
Oceans vast and shaded from green to deep blue full of life of it's own,
Animals of so many varieties we may never know the extent of their numbers:

How blessed we are that we are here on a world so beautiful,
Ever sharing with us that which you have given so generously,
From you we were created and to you we return when our time here is over,
To begin anew the cycle of life eternal within your bosom of love and warmth;

Once again that time of the year,
When cold winds blow and eyes do tear,
Colors start to show their face once again,
Yellows, Reds, Oranges shades begin;

As fall shows her colors from end to end,
Trees and bushes can now begin,
To show their beautiful hues,
Of changing over for all to view;

Amazing how the leaves are changing,
When their cycle is done and rearranging,
Hues of color so vivid and full,
Only to fall when they are through;

Soon the stems are all that's left,
A barren landscape of life has passed,
Snow will fall and cover them with its blanket,
To protect their roots from winters onset;

Somewhere in the night I knew,
That the darkness would fade away,
No longer would I wonder where to go,
Nor would I fear the shadows ever again;

Drifting aimlessly through this world without a goal,
Wandering down life's pathways seeking a way,
Looking for the one answer I sought so hard,
Why am I here and where will I go next;

Spent and weary I roamed the land,
Open to the fruits of labor and hardships of life,
Ever onwards without a goal I went,
Finding one closed door after another;

Never had I guessed that the open doorway would lead me here,
To the point in my life I am now faced with,
No fear or misunderstanding do I have,
For I am free to finally explore the totality of life;

In days before I was always afraid of making the wrong choices,
But now I know the right choice is here in front of me,
Following my heart and not my head I see where I should be,
Here with you and all that we have before us open and waiting;

All we have to do now is travel down this path,
Doors that were closed now open before us,
So much to see and comprehend on our journey,
Relieved that it is done and amazed at what lies ahead;

Forever onwards we go facing everything openly,
No more doubting what to do or where to go,
Free to learn and explore all that is life,
All that is love until the end of time is ours;

There's this girl named J I know,
Who's smile is lovely and laughter does flow,
Can be real sweet if you talk right,
Or give you down the road if you want a fight;

Takes the time to know who you are,
Will help you out if your near or far,
Does her job the best she can,
But doesn't like the grief you send;

She send's me all across this land,
To pick up freight and bring it in,
Works real hard to keep me right,
Moving loads both day and night;

Sometimes I see her on my way,
When passing through for just a day,
I'll stop and try to at least say hey!
Then once again I'm on my way;

Forever Your's!
For My Wife My Love!

We met in the spring of the very first year,
Rain coming down and cool in the air,
I walked into the store you were there,
I had noticed you then but had my own fear,

How quickly you brought my mind to ease,
With a beautiful smile warm as a summer breeze,
I felt the love in your soul and the joy in your eyes,
Finally found someone that wouldn't tell lies,

There seemed to be a bond from the very start,
Something told me from deep within my heart,
I had been in what I thought was love before,
But never had it been this intense or sure,

We talked and the words were unimportant,
We walked and we danced and became more confident,
After that it was only a matter of time,
I knew from then on that you would be mine,

Now even after thirty years of love,
I know that our love was made from above,
Nothing can ever change how I feel,
For nothing can destroy a love that is real!!

In the beauty of life there is one choice;
The choice of whom to love is one of course;
When children are born out of love;
They will grow strong and soar as a dove;

You first love your parents, who gave you life;
Then you learn about God, his love and strife;
This mighty of all from the heavens above;
Gave the life of his son, in the name of love;

As you grow into puberty, no longer a child;
You fall in love with someone loving and mild;
This love can be the most wondrous of all;
But choose carefully or your liable to fall;

To love one that's equal can be full of bliss;
For this kind of love means more than a kiss;
It's lasting and happy, with sorrow and joy;
True love can last between a Girl and a Boy;

As the years go by your hair turns to grey;
This you can count on to eternally stay;
The love you've known from the moment of birth;
Stays with you forever and you never will thirst!

Has the time grown near for the ending of mankind,
Or are we at the threshold for changes to be redefined,
If so then will we be ready to open new doorways,
Or confront that which is coming by running away;

How will we respond to the challenges ahead
Will our warring ways follow us until we're all dead
Or will we grow enough to stop all the killing
Finally living a life rewarding and fulfilling;

There will come a time when we have to face ourselves
How many will try to put their misdeeds on shelves
Face the truth and admit we're wrong to continue
Hurting and destroying within our own venue;

Blaming everyone else for our shortcomings and fears
Only worse off in the end as we're all shedding tears
Taking a step forward only to fall back three
So we never fall far from the family tree;

Try to believe with all of your might
Throughout your life that you done everything right
Be kind to each other and show that you care
Then the end of our days should be easy to bear;

How Long!
For My Loving Wife Now and Forever!!

How long in the darkness did I roam;
The very depths of despair did I go;
Yet no one was there to bring me home;
How I suffered through this to the final blow;

Clinging to nothingness of this life;
Then you came and took away the strife;
You gave me hope, where there was none;
You brought me out of darkness into the sun;

You took me into your heart and soul;
Gave me comfort and peace you did console;
Into the light of your wonderful smile;
Brought me back knowing all the while;

That I may not return your love;
You never gave up and searched above;
Not knowing how long before I could;
Because of others who had not been good;

Not afraid that I would stay or leave;
You continued giving and never grieved;
But I know there will never come that day;
For the rest of my life your love I'll repay!!

Has the time grown near for the ending of mankind,
Or are we at a threshold for changes to come in time?
If so, then will we be ready to open new doorways,
Or confront that which is coming our way.

How will we respond to new challenges?
Will our warring ways follow us to the end,
Or will we finally grow enough to stop.
Killing needlessly to prove who's right or wrong;

There has to come a time when we have to face ourselves.
How many will be able to confront what they've done,
Face the truth and admit we were wrong to continue.
Hurting and destroying that which others have built,

Blaming everyone for our shortcomings or fears,
Only to be worse off in the end, not proving anything.
Taking a step forward only to fall back three,
Awaken from the dream and see the truth or perish;

In the course of a lifetime where do we stand,
Walking into the dawn of a new day as a strand,
Of life that exist only to provide others with what they need,
We spend our days working for what some would term chicken feed:

Daily traversing the drive from our homes to place of work,
Spending hours behind desk although some try to shirk,
The task we perform cooking their food or making the snow,
Done by those of us who perform the task necessary to flow;

For those who don't care or try to show,
A simple thanks or who do you know,
Taken for granted by most in our path,
Till our lives are over and our time has passed;

Somewhere in the middle I know there's a chance,
Someone will care and take a second glance,
We may not seem important to all,
But if we stop the world could fall;

I know there are others just like me,
That feel their lives are dreary as can be,
But sometimes if only for a short while,
We can look out at others and give them a smile;

If only that is all we can give,
Perhaps it will be enough to help them to live,
Knowing that they are not alone in their task,
Along to another this smile they might pass;

Something so simple doesn't seem like much,
To people that feel there is no one to trust,
What if that smile you shared,
Showed someone that you cared;

A moment in passing with nothing to hide,
You can take a pleasure in this as you ride,
Back home to the life you know is waiting there,
With knowledge that someone's life could be spared;

Let The Music Flow!
For those who write music for all of us to enjoy!

How the music is in everything, even our very souls,
The rhythms of sound flooding outwards it flows,
Filling a sheet of paper with words or symbols,
Becoming a song full of love, grief, or left in limbo,

Thoughts drifting through in torrents of love,
Reaching out filled with joy or emotion as from above,
Drifting ever onwards to an endless sea to show,
A sea full of things brought forth from the soul,

Reaching out to others with our music of years,
Filling their void of emptiness or fears,
Giving them an outlet for their lives where they hide,
Giving meaning to what they feel deeply inside,

How simple it seems to be this gift,
Yet the words may come but does it lift,
The flow is it smooth, harsh, or happy,
The music may be good or sound sappy,

Whether reaching for the stars or getting down to earth,
Always there in our souls since the time of our birth,
To the outer bounds of our mind and onto the paper,
Ever flowing throughout the decades for all to savor!!

When did our society change,
From one that cared to one of shame,
There was a time when people cared,
Were glad to help with things they shared;

Gave freely from the heart to others,
The way they were taught by their mothers,
Took time for friends and neighbors too,
Spent time with all their families new;

Then something changed as they often do,
No longer having time for me and you,
Faster phones and dial-ups too,
To get things done quicker for me and you;

Fast food places and checkout lines,
Moving quickly became our times,
No time to see the world outside,
Too many things now to decide;

No time to stop and say hello,
Or listen to another's woe,
Our life moves quickly by,
Till the day comes when we die;

Then its quick and we're in the ground,
Hurry cause I'm from out of town,
Missing all the things in life that matter,
Quickly now the crowds do scatter;

No time to see to those in need,
We rush around always at full speed,
Have to get back to the place I live,
Sorry I haven't got the time to give;

In the beginning I was unsure that there would be a tomorrow,
Fears of all that I had lived for, coming to an end were in the open,
Uncertainty was ever present during these days of pain and loneliness,
Only when the surgery was over and I awakened did I know that it was O.K.;

Many days spent feeling helpless went by and nothing changed,
Worry over the outcome is sometimes worse than the actual happening,
We spend a lot of time rushing headlong into this world,
Never looking around or even looking back to see what we've missed;

How often we do not see the really important things in life,
Those who love us and want to take care of us no matter what,
The very sunrise of a new day or the sunset at days end,
The simple beauty that surrounds us in the world that is never hidden;

Yet we go through most of our lives being drawn into an abyss,
A place where we are too busy to see anything else around us,
Always rushing too and fro without turning our heads to see what's next to us,
Missing the best things in life as our children grow and the world changes;

Love is a hard thing to describe,
You can't see it when it comes to inscribe,
Feelings within you to show you've been grabbed,
That make you happy, sad, excited or mad,

A warm feeling overcomes you, not sure why,
Without reason it can make you cry,
Its depths can't be fathomed by words or sounds,
No probe could reach it or see it surround,

Your heart can feel it, those feelings abound,
With joy and happiness all around,
A whispered word, a gentle caress,
No other time are you filled with such happiness,

Its been felt by all, both old and young,
No method of science, not spread by tongue,
Or word of mouth from one to another,
Its felt by children for Father and Mother,

You feel it at the birth of a child,
Forever there with you feeling so proud,
But no matter what you say or you do,
No one can ever take these feelings from you!!

How beautiful the hills they lay,
All golden brown with crops of hay,
Distances unperceived by man,
How far they flow across the land;

Rivers flowing through deep gorge's,
Thru rocks from when the earth was formed
Canyons wide with deep steep sides,
Where these waters flow through country sides;

Land once untouched by man,
Has now turned into fertile land,
Where fruits and vegetables now do grow,
Upon what was once barren soil;

Land once hostile for all to view,
Turned into rich soil with life anew,
Where crops are grown and trees do grow,
Thanks to those who were in the know;

Amazed by how the land was changed,
Once broken lands now rearranged,
Smoothed out by the tools of man,
Created by their own two hands;

To take a land so bare and broken,
Turn it into one so full of life unspoken,
Growing plants where long before,
There was only barren waste and nothing more;

Mother!!

She gave us birth and nourished us
Taught us how to do for ourselves
Taught us how to talk and to listen
Gave us the strength to carry on.

Sat up with us when we were sick
Cared for us after a hard days work
Cooked, cleaned and washed our clothes
Never complaining about doing those chores.

Forever diligent in her efforts
To prepare us for a life of our own
Fighting for us when someone done us wrong
Punishing us for our wrong doing.

Teaching us always to do the right thing
Helping us with problems as they came up
Searching her memory for answers to questions
Showing us the best way to live our lives.

Never forgetting our birthdays even as we got older
Always there to assist when we needed help
No matter what time of day or night
Devoted to the fulfillment of that role as Mother!

Natures Echoes!
Dedicated to all those in and responsible for its creation!

I am the wave running against the shore did you hear me?
I began billions of years before just floating in darkness
I exploded in violence on your Island did you hear me?
In the beginning I raised myself up from the depths of the ocean

I encircle you everyday with warmth, cold, gentle and bold
Did you feel me on that summer night blowing through the trees?
Did you see me floating through the heavens above you?
Sometimes puffy wisp, sometimes giants in the air above

Did you hear me walking through your garden or calling for my mate?
Did you know me as I flew overhead on my journeys?
You touch me when you were a child or played on me through the years?
How many different names you have given me over the centuries?

Mother Earth, Gaia, Pearl of the Sky, Mother of All Creation
Through many generations have I watched you grow
I have echoed through your minds throughout eternity
Never far from your thoughts always in your soul;

From me you came and to me you shall return forever!

The evening Sun waning low over the horizon,
Shadows creeping slowly along the canyon floor,
Ever so slowly winding their way up the walls they flow,
Carrying the daylight ahead of them as they go;

Darkness envelopes the landscape as if all things will end,
Foreboding takes control as I move over the sand,
Seeking a familiar landmark or some sort of guide,
I search through the darkness for some sort of life;

Finally reaching the end of day the shadows move on,
Fading light lingering on in the edges of the sky,
Wisp of clouds float gently by as breezes slowly stir,
A star burst through as a beacon light to guide all anew;

Then slowly ever so slowly they begin to appear,
Easing my anxiety, spirits laid to rest I can settle back,
Once again awaiting the beginning of a brand new day,
When all things start anew in all their splendor as the new day is born;

How wonderful it is that life has given me a chance,
To bring forth the thoughts and experiences of life past,
To transform the things in life I see,
Into Poetry for all the world to read;

There is so much in everyday that people just ignore,
The changes in our daily lives they never seen before,
Weather changes year to year and no one pays attention,
Until they are swept up into it and caught up in the tension;

The constant threat of war that beckons to begin,
Where once again we know that we will loose our men,
Fighting on some foreign soil to try to make things right,
Even though there are those who think it not our fight;

How are we to make the choice for others in distress,
We live in constant turmoil even amongst ourselves,
Street gangs killing one another for no real reason,
Drive by shootings without a care to the children they are killing;

Children killing children in our schools is all the rage,
Once again reminding us that we need to turn the page,
How long ago these things did happen in the past,
How we've forgotten what we though just could not last;

Our country has tried so hard to repress,
The problems in our homeland no one wants to address,
People out of work and living in the streets,
Looking for someone to help them in their time of need;

Worrying about a celebrity that has to go to jail,
While everything around them is going all to hell,
What has our society come to when its gotten to this point,
That nothings as important than a famous persons plight;

Its not the first won't be the last for everyone to see,
Just wait a little while and turn on your T.V.,
I guess its just the way that the media you see,
Is trying to take our minds off the troops we have overseas;

How much time you spend on the floor walking back and forth
Listening for someone to whimper or call out for you
Some working in the ER some in maternity or other areas
Always there to give of yourselves no matter how you feel,

Learning new task for the jobs you have already
Putting up with the good and not so good patients
Hovering over them as a mother over her children
Facing every obstacle for those you take care of,

From major problems of life and death to the simple cold
Never giving up you put yourself out there every day
If I only have one smile it is for you in hopes
That maybe you will be able to share it with others,

Then getting home to loved ones after a rough day
All of you working together to take care of us during your day
How thankful I am for having met you and the treatment you gave me,
Day or night you're the family there when everyone is gone,

I thank each and everyone of you for your devotion,
To your jobs, families, and those of us who where under your care,

You stood there so proud for scores of years;
Providing shade and a place for tears;
Your branches reaching towards the sky;
Giving shelter from storms to passers by;

How gracefully you swayed in the breeze;
So effortlessly you moved with such ease;
A nesting place for fowls of all breeds;
Providing them with shelter as well as seeds;

You upheld swings hung on your branches;
Took the brunt of blows and rock glances;
Lasted far longer than many others;
Put up with all the children and Mothers;

You grew to the greatest height at last;
Only to lose your life in one blast;
Came a storm with thunder and lightning;
It scared everyone for it was so frightening;

In an instant of lightning flash so bright;
It lit up the sky in the darkening night;
Cut down by the most powerful element of all;
Was your time when this storm made you fall!!

I guess I had never given thought to how much things have gone by,
I can remember a time before color television or portables,
Before computers, DSL's, Satellite dish's or cell phones,
When a pay phone only cost a dime to call around town,

Cartoons that were funny, not fighting creatures or warriors,
When playing ball meant baseball, not giving in,
Soda Pop was a dime and five cents of that was the deposit,
When a dollar in your hand made you feel good,

When drive-ins were for movies or a favorite A&W Root Beer stand,
Where everyone met after school without being harassed,
A time when drugs or bringing guns to school didn't happen,
When the drug dealers were the doctors and pharmacists for medicine,

When you could lay down at night with your windows open,
Never locking your doors during the day or night,
I remember when cars lasted the lifetime of parents and children,
Homes were built where your land was, not brought in sections,

When being a man of your word, meant you kept it,
Why it was a lifetime of love, and the love of a lifetime,
How many years does it take to change these things,
Forty years prior, but it could all change again tomorrow!!

Today there was a silence that no one could break
The air was still, and heat unbearable to all
A soft breeze began to blow ever so slightly
Bringing a little relief from the suns burning rays;

Small clouds began to fill the sky
Casting their shadow as they pass by
Playing over the landscape in unusual patterns
Some forming shapes of animals and objects;

How much we could see in these clouds as children
Without doubt the images we could see without burden
As time goes by less attention we pay
Forgetting all the things of kids at play;

So much enjoyed as children forgotten as adults
Games played and forgotten insults
Sharing with everyone having fun was all that mattered
No fears or concerns from life to drag us down;

A much simpler life as children without cares
No one to worry over or to bring you grief
Problems of this world didn't bear down on us
How carefree those times were a memory to share;

All things that are were before, and will be again
We shall all become as children again before we die
Such will become the way of the world in the end of time
For we shall all have to answer for what we have done;

From snow covered mountains you slowly wind,
Through cracks and earth you seep,
Ever relentless in your quest to join the rest,
Of the waters flowing from the heavens weep;

Ever so slowly at first you appear,
As wisp of water falling from a leaf so near,
From a trickle to a babbling brook as it travels on,
To become a stream of water pure and clean;

On down the mountains you pick up speed,
As you are joined by other various feeds,
Of waters spawned from other points on high,
Your waters now flowing so swiftly by;

Over boulders you begin to cascade down mountains,
Gaining speed over rapids sometimes making fountains,
Always gaining more power as you flow towards your final goal,
Through long forgotten valleys and hills do you roam;

A mighty river now you've become providing water for all in the sun,
To your edge do they explore the boundaries of your shore,
Your waters they use to grow crops and on the plains their fruits and grains,
Animals from far and near come to refresh anew;

You meander on through hills and plains,
Past towns and cities where it has rained,
Though canyon lands into desert under open sky,
Flowing into oceans that seem endless to the eye;

Seek for all the things in life that matter,
Not the material things but the spiritual,
Seek not the things that create hate,
But the things that bring joy into your lives;

Endeavor to become one with the world,
In turn the world will become one with you,
Never give up seeking things in your life,
For there is power in knowledge not strife,

Look for the good in all things,
You will find it truly rings,
Reaching outwards towards the heavens above,
It will come back to you with love,

Find the will to carry on,
That which brings you to the dawn,
Of a soul not bound by man,
Then you'll be known throughout the land!!

Pre dawn hours, streets are deserted,
Perfumed smell of flowers permeate the air,
Sun glinting off the windows of houses in the morn,
Does show the beauty of your city in the dawning;

Not huge like larger cities I have seen,
Just small communities some never seen,
By travelers who follow normal roads and routes,
To their destination of community or house;

The beauty of your houses, mostly old and some are new,
Presents us with a feeling of a place where we once grew,
Before a time of chaos, before the time of war,
Back to a time of no worries like children at the door;

Where people didn't worry about locks upon the door,
No barred windows to protect their very store,
How nice it was to visit you, if only for awhile,
For you bring back sweet memories, that bring about a smile;

It's good to know that no matter how bad things may seem,
There's always a place where we can go to sit beside a stream,
Listen to the quiet and really be at peace knowing that its safe,
Not waiting for the world to end at some ungodly pace;

How lovely the flowers do grow from the earth,
Bringing forth all the colors of the rainbow,
For all of us to enjoy and smell,
As their fragrance permeates the air;

Roses, Lilacs, Bluebells and more,
Free for all to see and adore,
How they bring such joy,
When given by a girl or boy;

What person doesn't employ this wonder of nature,
To please one they love and adore,
How simple a thing can be and yet,
It grows and we pick it without regret;

The warmth of the sun now shines anew,
Springtime bringing forth life to view,
Warming the earth and all of us too,
We feel refreshed as born anew;

How it must feel as a newborn child,
Thrust out in the world so wild,
To be brought out of a mothers womb,
Into the light of a cold, cold room;

Bright lights glaring down from above,
Prodded and cleaned they can't feel the love,
Crying for whatever reason as if to say,
Why are you doing this to me today,

Peace at last as the bond begins,
When child and parents are together again,
Can you envision what must transpire,
As this child conceived wonders who you are;

Teach them well as they grow,
All the things they will need to know,
Not the stuff they learn in school,
But how to live by the golden rule;

No matter hard you try you might,
Pass on the things you don't like,
Hatred of others and fear of some,
For the things in life they have done;

How quickly they learn to read and write,
But quicker they learn how to hate and to fight,
We can only try to do what's right,
And teach them love for all in sight;

Maybe someday when we all grow,
Our children will show us what they know,
That there is a place for all to live,
That is from the heart for all to give;

The wind blew by my window sill
Brisk at the beginning of a new day
Birds were singing in the trees
Children playing in the leaves

Once again fall has come to our town
When the leaves turn amber and brown
All the colors of natures rainbow
Softly falling to the ground

Faintly an echo in the distance
Lets me know that a storm is sure to grow
Blowing swiftly across the plains
Thunder and lightning then the rains

Quickly it passes fading into the distance
No hills or mountains for resistance
Just as the memories of our childhood go
Rushing through those years like a storm does blow

Maturing quickly to be on our own
To raise a family and buy a home
My how quickly the years do go
Our hair now the color of snow!!

I sit in the night listening to the silence but there is none,
The dog barking in the distance, crickets chirping, wind in the trees,
All these things there to remind me I'm never alone,
Distant thunder, or voices carried on the wind,

The day done the sounds of the night become clearer,
No noise of traffic, or planes overhead to disrupt thought,
Deeper into the night I go and the sounds grow fainter,
As if being transported to another place,

No longer bound to the world of daytime with its hurried sounds,
Free from the sounds that can overwhelm the soul,
Your very senses can feel the changes as you struggle on,
A shooting star appears from no where and you gaze upon it in wonder,

Where from the heavens did you come on your long journey,
What sites you must have seen, birth and death of new worlds and old,
Great spinning masses like our own Solar System,
Life reaching for the stars such as we hope to do some day,

When we venture out there will we have the compassion to do it right,
Or will we carry our ways with us that are not so peaceful,
Seeking not only to explore new worlds but to conquer them?
Perhaps that's why we have not achieved this goal till we're ready!!!

Is this the dawning of a new age, or a repeat of days gone by;
Do we live in an era of totally new creation;
Or simply things that have been before in a forgotten past;
Is there really anything that hasn't been done before;

What has brought mankind to believe any knowledge is new;
We know that this world is several billion years old;
Yet we cannot acknowledge that man could be that old;
We live, dream, love, hope, and die never knowing this could be;

That everything we have now, could have been before;
In another time and place in our distant past;
Our homes, cities, countries, all could have been before;
Only to have been erased by time and start anew;

We've sat upon the threshold of annihilation in our own time;
In our history is many a time mankind has come close;
We cannot be content to accept one another for our beliefs;
Thereby creating a reason to wage war one upon another;

Are we so perfect in our beliefs that we do these things?
I think not, for that which we believe to be true of others;
Is usually the way we become to defeat them in all our glory;
We accomplish nothing but to destroy ourselves in the end!

The Week Before X-Mas!
No harm meant!

Was the week before Christmas and in all the malls,
The Santa's were busy within there great walls,
They sat in their chairs for all to see,
For so many children to sit on their knee,

A picture for Mommy, one for an Aunt,
Another for Grandma the photographer chants,
Oh look how excited the kids seem to be,
Some laughing some frowning while on Santa's knee,

How happy the shopkeepers seem as they smile,
Customers roaming about in each brand new isle,
They know in their hearts that the weeks end will bring,
Great tidings of comfort, more cash in the spring,

Please take your time, take as long as you want,
He says to the people with presents to hunt,
I'm sure that you'll find it that one special gift,
If not then just tell me it'll be on next years list,

The shoppers all through now the Santa's at ease,
Can finally go home and soak their poor knees,
The stores in the mall are closed and locked tight,
The owners say Merry Christmas to All,

How deep must we search before we see,
The fear from things others have done,
Despair and sorrows on the verge,
Building up in us until they surge.

Lashing outwards towards those we fear,
Giving thought to the things that we hear,
Only despair for those we cannot console,
Things so far out of our own control.

How many must suffer, how many must die,
Reaching out for the enemy from the sky,
A land so destroyed by those before,
Once more must face the wrath of a Nation at war.

A war against those who we learn to abhor,
Through the worst possible way they destroy from the core,
They eat at our hearts with disgust and revenge,
Till we wish to destroy them and put it to an end.

Be careful my fellow man and don't get confused,
They will destroy without feeling and always abuse,
The freedoms we have in this land of our own,
Hard fought throughout time here we try not to lose!

The oceans mighty roar, as I left the California shore,
To begin my search across the land, America so grand,
Over the mountains, across the plains,
Traveled the misty mountains glory, to the desert down below;

Past the golden fields of wheat, waving like the ocean in the wind,
Growing strong through the pouring rains,
Driving on through valley's so wide, could not see the other side,
Continuing on through the cornfields, of the central states;

Winding roads and small foothills, into the mountains of the blue ridge,
Peaks not as high as those in the west, but with a beauty not to be missed;
Flowing outwards into hills, towards the eastern shores,
Where battles once raged through our Civil War;

Towards the beaches, where rivers flow into the ocean forevermore,
There to receive the rush of the waves, which come and shape the shore,
So much beauty to behold, throughout this land as it unfolds,
We listened as children, as their stories were told;

Those who came before us, to this land of light and glory,
Seeking a place to bring their families, and start anew,
Spreading out all across this great wide land,
To make this the greatest country in the world for all who come here to live.

Poetry comes from the heart ,
At times its sad or full of warmth.
Feelings that you have for someone you love or have lost.
Emotions that you have felt and thought lost.

Sometimes things that you cannot explain ,
When writing them out becomes very plain.
There doesn't have to be a rhyme or reason ,
You can even write about the seasons.

Inner most thoughts or feelings,
When put to paper make up your reasons.
Past events that you've been through,
Becomes a way to see you through.

There are those who can't seem to write ,
In the way a poet finds delight.
Things that seem to come and go ,
Forgotten dreams or friend's long ago.

Freely sit and try to express ,
Things that brought joy or distress.
Always leave an open mind ,
To things you've seen or left behind.

Poetry is not a way of writing to me,
But a way to keep myself in harmony.
With all the things in life I may see,
Trees and mountains, flowers, and bees.

Let your heart always be your guide,
Through life's ups and downs and keep your pride.
The words will fill your mind and astound you,
With expressive sights that are all around you.

Freely write what you feel at the time,
Not trying to make a poem that rhymes.
Words that come from deep inside,
Will help you find the ones that rhyme.

Write about things you know,
Like wind and rain or falling snow.
Think about your childhood years,
Write about your joys or fears.

But most of all try to remember,
The things in life you've had to surrender.
For those are the ones that shape and guide you,
They are feelings carried deep inside you.

As I looked out my window at the frost upon the ground;
I wondered if each crystal had a thought;
A glimpses of that which was ahead at daylight;
When the warming of the sun began to vaporize them;

Then as quickly my mind drifted on to other things;
The day ahead full of new and wondrous sights;
Places to visit that I had not seen before;
People to greet and discuss life with;

The dawn of a new day brings forth a new perspective;
For there is always something new to see or learn;
If you look deep within yourself you will find new things;
Just as the variations in each snowflake so are our lives;

No matter what every day is different in some way;
It may seem like the same boring task or job;
But there is always something new to discover;
Believe that you have nothing to learn you won't;

Believe that the world is full of new and wondrous things;
You will find something you never knew about;
Live each day as a child, learning about their world;
The world around you will show you all her glory!!!

Why do we torture ourselves on a daily basis in our lives,
Always searching for a better way or plan to achieve our strives,
Ever forward into the vast unknown of our emotions,
Looking for the one thing that will give us our devotions,

Where will it end in the vastness of that which is us,
Our depths cannot be found in this lifetime till we are dust,
Into the bowels of our soul do we search for that which is a must,
Never understanding that which is fast reaching towards lust,

Surrender to the truth of where we are now in this time,
Put those thoughts that mean the most down in rhyme,
Passages of dreams that others may have a chance to see,
There is a chance for all of us to be full of prophecy,

Describe how your heart has passed the pressures of this life,
How through your writings you overcame those stresses and strife,
Flowing throughout the ages of man and realizing above all,
That you found the answer within your soul in order to stand tall!

Scattered thoughts where are you leading me,
Adrift in the void of my mind to be,
Brought out in words and ideas to the eye of my mind,
To be written or spoken in ways of our time,

Looking, searching in the depths of my soul,
Seeking an outlet so that you can flow,
From the inner most reaches you wind your way,
To the outside you come no more time for play,

How great it is to be made manifest,
How long it took to get here is only to guess,
There's so much to see and so much to do,
How quickly you sort out the things that are new,

Restless we roam through this pathway called life,
Trying to give the best without strife,
Hoping to help others find their way,
To the dawning of a brand new day!!!

Dream that special dream in your soul that reaches for the heavens above,
Remember that which you love dearly to hold on to that one true love,
Never surrender your heart to whimsical or fanciful things,
Love one another as you want to be loved, fully without strings;

Live your life loving each other as if you don't have enough time,
As if there is a chance your life could end from a crime,
Spend each hour with each other in total fullness of that love,
Be sure to express it to those around you everyday far above;

Reach out with your heart to those around you,
Shower them with love let your heart be true,
Find it in your heart to share all the love you possibly can,
Openly and freely show them all the love of a special friend;

Never doubt your feelings about those you meet,
Always give freely and never retreat,
They will always remember that one special someone who gave them time,
Passing on to others what you've shown them within their own lifetime;

If you think it doesn't matter what you think or do,
There is always a chance it could happen to you,
A day will come when your sad feeling blue,
Someone will be there to help you through;

Go forth in the world as if each day is the last,
Be ready to forget the pains of the past,
You'll always be remembered as the only one,
Who shared life with feeling and enjoyed the sun;

The winds were ever gently on the night before
Caressing the trees so softly as they often had before
As the twilight lingered the sky began to change
Grey clouds started forming faster came the winds;

Darker ever darker the sky's began to show
Another storm brewing like I've never seen before
Lightning flashes cross the sky and some upon the ground
Dust and things blowing from places all around;

A whisper only of what was to come from those clouds overhead
When spirals of clouds appeared and headed for the ground
Winds harshly blowing now like nothing else before
Tearing up the trees and slamming at the door;

Sounds like a freight train multiplied four fold
Growing so intense as to take your very soul
Screaming cross the landscape destroying everything
Nothing in its pathway where it roams could be safe;

Trees bending in the wind as the funnel passes near
Bits of houses, cars and trees falling all around
Swiftly as it came now the storm continues on
Heading on across the land destroying everyone;

How quickly now the sounds subside and quietly it gets
A funnel cloud has passed us and our house it missed
But as I look out of my door to take a look around
There is so much debris from other places laying on the ground;

I search around for others to try and assist
Hoping as I wander round that all my friends it missed
How hard it is to envision a scene such as this
Many times repeated and the loved ones that are missed;

How long has it been now since we first came to this great land,
Odd that there were native people in this country before us,
Living in harmony with the land and all of God's creations,
Helping those of us who came over here to live to survive;

Peaceful by nature unless provoked to defend their lands,
Same as any of us would do even now in this day and age,
Yet we kept coming and drove them from their lands,
Ever expanding our realm until they took a stand against us;

How many American Indians we destroyed I do not know,
We warred against them till there was nothing left for them,
Took away their lands and way of life and called them savages,
They were the only true Americans and yet they have no rights;

How could that have made us better than them by what we did,
They lived with the land never taking what they didn't put back,
Where we have destroyed the land and polluted the rivers,
Leveled mountains for the minerals and chemicals for our use;

All for progress and the betterment of mankind?
Really doesn't add up in the final analysis does it.
Locked away on reservations the Indians are not allowed to vote,
The majority of them living in poverty for centuries under our rule;

Yet we condemn other countries for treating their people that way,
Have we not done the same if not worse to those who belong here,
Oppression of a race of people who should be praised,
For they gave back whatever they took from the earth;

I know that those who began this quest did not foresee the end,
What gave our forefathers the right to destroy their people and culture,
Force them from their lands and browbeat them into submission,
How would anyone today like it if another country did it to us?

I know that we can never return what was taken by force,
But there should be some gratitude to them for the sacrifices they made,
To survive as a race of people still regarded as not belonging,
In a land they once claimed as their own and shared with us;

The dawn came and went,
Then the darkness moved in,
No one knew what that would bring,
For it was something new to them.

They had emerged from a deep sleep,
From so many dreams of what they believed,
Never really facing the truth,
Never knowing there was anything else.

They had walked the pathway of life in their dreams,
But that was another reality, in another time,
Following well worn trails through this existence,
As a new born does through trial and resistance.

Then something happened to open this portal,
Time became a real feature of life for them,
No more could they wander aimlessly through a perfect world,
That had stayed the same dawn after dawn.

They had been awakened from this dream into a world of chaos,
Their lives ever changed by what was presented to them,
For the world they once knew is no more,
The comforts they had, gone forever in time.

They awakened into a world of cruel and unknown perils,
No one to protect them from the way things really are,
No one to take the blame for their mistakes any longer,
Seeing for the first time they had created what they no longer knew.

A world gone from perfect peace, which no one can have,
To the reality that their world was taken from them,
By the very powers they had endowed those that were chosen,
They had brought the creation of all things to the ultimate.

Bringing about the creation of bigger and better weapons,
Quicker and more deadly than the other,
Until there was nothing left to destroy,
Not a living thing left alive in this realm.

A planet once abundant with life no longer remained,
Blue skies above lands of mountains and streams,
Filled with oceans of water from dark blue into greens,
All destroyed by fighting war's never to shine anymore;

A glimmer of hope that mankind would survive,
But even at that would they change their designs,
How many times repeated before this saga of man,
Only to fall by the wayside and start fighting again;

Will there ever come a time when we try once again,
To present ourselves to the powers at hand,
Prove that we've learned what we need to know,
That all life is precious and learn war to abhor;

Only the rising of the moon and the sun were there,
Looking down on a barren planet where life was before,
Only then did they realize that they had gone too far,
Giving far to much knowledge can be deadly to all.

Believing that no one would misuse this power,
Was by far the biggest mistake of all,
Believing that no one needed to be there to guide them,
That they could ignore things that were there besides them.

To show them how to use and control this knowledge,
Most of all to teach them the love and compassion,
That all living things that were created,
Are necessary to everyone's existence;

So now there is nothing left of this perfect world,
No! This became a world of imperfectness instead,
Finding out too late that someone needed to show they cared,
Someone needed to live in the midst,
Guide them, teach them and love them.

Has the time come for our country to fall
There are those who think so without recall
Deficits from all administrations
Will it lead to our own suffocation;

Each generation has swore that it would end
Only to face it all once again and again
Promises made and promises broken
Given out like nothing more than a token;

Wars arise and again we fight
To give them freedom from their plight
Always falling back they go
To the very way they were before;

Wasted time and wasted life
Given up in all our strife
Free them teach them all in vane
For they cannot exist unless in pain;

Yet our country must go on
Continue fighting till we're done
To give them what we think they want
Only to come back on us to haunt;

Attacks against us both real or feared
Has caused us all to be afraid
For what will happen in the end
When we're depleted and have no friends;

Resources down, cost at an all time high
Yet our country squeezes by
Struggling hard to understand
Just how much it cost this land;

Where will this problem lead who knows
But troops are sent and the problem grows
These places afar where our troops do go
To try and fight an unseen foe;

Its been this way since the first world war
To end all wars was the thing they swore
Didn't turn out the way they said
More and more of our troops are dead;

These other lands have been at war
For at least two thousand years or more
How can we began to convince
Everyone to look at it from our side of the fence;

Just how many troops must die
Before the world has passed us by
Caring not if we're left in the cold
If our country should ever fold;

Once again that time of year ,
When cards are sent to bring some cheer,
Express a love or friendship dear,
To another shared through the year;

Poems do come in vast array,
To celebrate this special day,
Such a feeling shared for hours,
Gifts of candy and of flowers;

Showering someone special with a gift,
In hopes of getting at least a kiss,
A sign of your true affection,
Waiting to see if you'll be rejected;

What starts as children in school,
Will follow us our whole life through,
To just remember this time of year,
A Valentine for My Love so Dear;

Every year since man came into being I've been here,
Waiting patiently for an opening through fear,
Knowing that sooner or later I'd get my chance,
To come rushing in headlong without a second glance;

Don't know when it first began but it only takes two,
Whether it's two countries or two religions matters not,
Whenever there is discontent I can get a foot in the door,
Creating havoc is easy when you've done it so many times before;

For thousands of years I've been around,
Getting better each time at fear and sounds,
Making people want what others have or take it,
Never caring how much it cost or how many will die;

In the early years it was fighting hand to hand,
Then came clubs and spears to take man down,
Quickly now it progressed to men on horseback with swords,
Then on to guns of all sizes and shapes came the word;

On to armored vehicles and bigger trucks to haul more men,
Airplanes to fly them in and strafe the columns once again,
Then came bombs all bigger and better than their foe,
Never caring if it killed service or civilian just let them go;

With each generation you improved your fighting skills,
Creating better weapons to speed up your kills,
Shells fired from cannons and bombs dropped from the air,
Became easier and easier to wipe out large numbers without a care;

The next thing to appear so powerful a thing to cause great fear,
Atomic fusion more powerful than anything else did finally appear,
What a great weapon you finally made to send millions to their graves,
One bomb could now do what thousands couldn't and you still craved;

So a rocket you created to deliver this and more,
A hundred times faster then ever before,
Now everyone has them and no one is mad,
But if it should happen you better be sad;

For all that this world has withstood in the past,
Will come to an end with one final big blast,
Pray for our children and their children too,

That this just won't happen because of me and you;

Peace is the answer if mankind is to live,
Or there will be nothing left for our children to give,
Make sure that you teach them to love all mankind,
No matter what color, religion, beliefs or design!!!

How long will it be now, no-one can be sure,
For so many years there was a feeling of life so pure,
Never changing from one moment till the next,
Feeling as though it would go on never be hexed;

Things can change quickly when one becomes too sure,
That nothing in life or family could ever become obscure,
A blink of an eye is a lifetime in a moment of distress,
Never ending struggles with what is right and best;

No secure feelings could ever be replaced by a longing to be loved,
That is a feeling one can only get answered from above,
A loving touch, a warm embrace, a whispered word of prayer,
That's what you brought to me with your loving care;

Without you by my side to show your love and grace,
My life would have been an empty shell and a very lonely place,
You've brought me love and peace deep down in my soul,
For without your love I'd have no life or goal;

Forever you'll be with me for now and evermore,
By finding you my soul mate and opening up that door,
I know that from this moment on no-one could take your place,
For you have showed love and tenderness that can never be replaced;

No matter what the future holds my love for you shall always remain,
Throughout the days we have left, our love will never change,
Believe and I will be there even when my life is past,
For you are my one true love throughout eternity will last;

I walk your streets alone, a wanderer in the night,
Searching for a doorway that has a warming light,
Silently I stand there and knock upon your door,
Waiting for an answer as I've done many times before;

No one comes to answer as they look out through their screens,
They see a weary traveler and the fears that it brings,
I did not come to harm you or to lead you astray,
I came to bring you guidance to a better way;

Courtyards all empty, steps clean and bare,
Hillsides barren cause no one seems to care,
How sadly I remember the days gone by before,
When laughter filled the air from the crowds mighty roar;

I was alone then just as I am right now,
Awaiting someone to believe in me somehow,
That everything I'd done had not been in vain,
To show the world a better way, not suffering in pain;

Not to travel through this life being harmful to each other,
But to share what we've been given with one another,
Peace for your soul is all that I can give,
If this is the life that you choose to live;

Just believe in God above, his willingness to forgive,
Not carry all the hatred of others to the grave,
Find it in our hearts to settle all the pain,
Of wanting what the others had worked so hard to gain;

How cold the wind has become as the day lingers on,
Pilling high the snow does climb to cover all the countryside,
Clouds of gray go floating by dropping snowflakes from the sky,
Pure and clean, white as can be, fun at times for you and me,

In this snow the children play as we once did back in the day,
Building Snowmen /Sledding /Ice Skating and Skiing for play,
Laying down upon the ground to make an angle so profound,
How fun it was to be a child and play outside upon the ground,

As we grow so does the way we think of snow in a different way,
Shoveling/Driving/Working too its not such fun for me and you,
Its funny how our opinions change as life goes by and we do age,
From fun to burden so it seems this winter chill we hold to blame,

Our bodies now reflect the pain of playing outside in the cold,
Hours and hours of outside fun becomes harder as we get old,
Working in this wintry mix is not as fun at fifty six,
Sure will be glad when winters done cause soon I'll be sixty one;

In the hours ahead I'm filled with dread waiting through the night,
I wait to see the dawning and the suns precious light,
Feelings of despair prevail as though I've fallen in a well,
Where whispers can be heard yet not a word I understood;

Worlds collide and stars are born and yet the void continues on,
Into darkness I still fall unable to see or hear your call,
Caressed by the darkness I continue on waiting for this dream to end,
A light which will bring such splendor so my heart can surrender;

A flight of birds flies overhead and brings me out of the dread,
No longer fearful of what could be, I awaken in my bed,
To realize for one more day, I'll be here to enjoy your ways,
In my heart I always knew that it would be just me and you;

As I awaken from this dream, I know that you are close to me,
Always there when I'm in need, with a kiss or smile so sweet,
So happy am I that we met, fell in love as if planned from above,
Your sparkling eyes and loving touch show me daily of your love;

About The Author!

I was born in Evansville, Indiana on Nov.3,1946, raised in Chicago, Ill. Where I went into the Navy at 17 and spent time in Viet Nam on an amphibious craft. Came home and began my life as anyone would to provide their self with the necessities of life. Have written a lot over the years never kept the poetry I had written on napkins or placemats. Gave them away mostly so I do not know what happened with those poems. Hope someone got enjoyment from them at least. I now live in Martinsville, Va. where I met my wife of 30 years and raised 5 children together. Only regret I guess would be that I didn't have all the poetry I've written over the years. Please enjoy what you read and keep an open mind to everything in life you see and love for it will always be there. I hope to keep writing as long as I am able and want all who read these poems to openly express your feelings about what you think and feel about them.

Robert L. Fox

www.ingramcontent.com/pod-product-compliance
Lightning Source LLC
aVergne TN
HW081321060426
509LV00015B/1617

* 9 7 8 0 6 1 5 1 8 5 8 9 7 *